# Strange Eating Habits of Sea Creatures

# Strange Eating Habits of Sea Creatures

Jean H. Sibbald

Dillon Press, Inc.
Minneapolis, Minnesota 55415

*The photographs are reproduced through the courtesy of Charles Arneson, John A.K. Davies, the National Oceanic and Atmospheric Administration, Jeff Rotman, James Rowan, and Lynn Stone. Cover photo: a damselfish swims among the colorful tropical waters of a coral reef. (Charles Arneson)*

Library of Congress Cataloging in Publication Data

Sibbald, Jean H.
  Strange eating habits of sea creatures.
  (Ocean world library)
  Bibliography: p.
  Includes index.
  Summary: Examines the eating habits of several sea creatures, pointing out their interdependence on each other.
  1. Marine fauna—Food—Juvenile literature. 2. Marine ecology—Juvenile literature. [1. Marine animals—Food. 2. Marine ecology] I. Title. II. Series.
  QL122.2.S58  1986      591.5'2636      85-11621
  ISBN 0-87518-349-2

Dillon Press, Inc., 242 Portland Avenue South
Minneapolis, Minnesota 55415

Printed in the United States of America
1 2 3 4 5 6 7 8 9 10 95 94 93 92 91 90 89 88 87 86

# Contents

Sea Facts . . . . . . . . . . . . . . . . . . . . . . . . 7

Introduction . . . . . . . . . . . . . . . . . . . . . . 9

1 Filter Feeders . . . . . . . . . . . . . . . . . . . . 13

2 Grazers . . . . . . . . . . . . . . . . . . . . . . . . . 23

3 Gulpers . . . . . . . . . . . . . . . . . . . . . . . . . 32

4 Biters and Slashers . . . . . . . . . . . . . . . 37

5 Drillers and Hammerers . . . . . . . . . . . 47

6 Fishers . . . . . . . . . . . . . . . . . . . . . . . . . 54

7 Farmers . . . . . . . . . . . . . . . . . . . . . . . . 59

8 Shockers . . . . . . . . . . . . . . . . . . . . . . . 64

9 Poisoners . . . . . . . . . . . . . . . . . . . . . . . 68

10 Guests—Friendly and Unfriendly . . . . 79

11 Pinchers and Crawlers . . . . . . . . . . . . . 86

Appendix A: Learning More About
                Sea Life . . . . . . . . . . . . .   93
Appendix B: Scientific Names for
                Sea Animals . . . . . . . .   95
Glossary . . . . . . . . . . . . . . . . . . . . . .   100
Selected Bibliography . . . . . . . . . . . . .   106
Index . . . . . . . . . . . . . . . . . . . . . . . . .   109

 *Sea Facts*

**Size:**

140,000,000 square miles (361,000,000 square kilometers)—71 percent of the earth's surface

**Different Species of Sea Animals:**

About 160,000

**Different Species of Seaweeds (Algae):**

About 10,000

**Foods for Sea Animals:**

*Filter feeders*—plant and animal plankton
*Grazers and farmers*—seaweeds (algae)
*Drillers and hammerers*—shellfish
*Gulpers, biters, fishers, shockers, poisoners, guests, pinchers, and crawlers*—various sea animals

**Smallest Foods for Sea Animals:**

*Plant plankton*—0.001 to 0.04 inch (0.025 to 1 millimeter)
*Animal plankton*—0.04 to 0.2 inch (1 to 5 millimeters)

**Largest Foods for Sea Animals:**

*Plant, giant kelp*—up to 200 feet (61 meters) long
*Animal, blue whale*—110 feet (33.5 meters) long, 150 tons (135 metric tons) in weight

 *Introduction*

Sea creatures, like all animals, must have food to live. But just as life in the sea is much different than life on land, so eating in the sea is different than eating on land.

The food itself is different. It swims, floats, gets tossed about by waves and tides, is buried in the sand, or is hidden in hard shells. It ranges in size from **microscopic**,* or too tiny to see, to larger than a semi-trailer. It includes most creatures of the sea, for almost all are food for others. In fact, life in the sea is often a matter of eat and be eaten.

Sea creatures obtain their food in many ways. Many must catch it on the run or, more accurately, on the swim. Some must strain their food out of the water, capturing it in their own special filters or sieves. Some drill through hard shells to reach the soft meat hidden inside. Others scrape tiny plants from the surface of rocks. Some sea creatures slash, attack, or bite. Others gulp their food. Some even raise their own food.

The feeding process follows a pattern. Certain types of sea life serve as food for others, which are, in turn, food for others, which are themselves eaten. Each of these feeding groups forms a link in the **food**

*Words in **bold type** are explained in the glossary at the end of this book.

*Barracudas are sea carnivores, or meat eaters.*

**chain**. Each link depends for its existence on the link before it.

The food chain begins with plant life—the food producers. Plants use the light of the sun together with water, **minerals**, and **carbon dioxide** to make food. In the sea, there are seaweeds of many sizes. By far the most abundant are tiny **algae** that drift about unseen. Together with animals, just as small, they make up the **plankton**, a vast, drifting sea pasture. So numerous are these tiny **organisms** that a quart of seawater will contain as many as a million of them.

The animal plankton eat the plant plankton. In this way they form the second link of the food chain. Some **shellfish** and other small creatures are also part of this link because they, too, feed on the plant plankton. Plant eaters are called **herbivores**, or herbivorous animals.

Next in the chain come the small fish that eat the animal plankton, and sometimes the plant plankton as well. Almost all baby fish fit in this group since plankton is their baby food. Bottom-dwelling fish, starfish, and some snails are also part of this group because they eat herbivores such as shellfish.

Then come larger fish to feed upon the smaller

*Giant kelp is the largest seaweed in the ocean.*

fish. The large fish are, in turn, food for the largest meat eaters, such as the sharks and killer whales.

The meat eaters are called **carnivores**, or carnivorous animals. Creatures that eat both meat and plants are **omnivores**, or omnivorous animals.

There are some surprises in the food chain. You would expect the largest animal in the sea to eat the next-largest animal in the sea. But the blue whale, the largest animal in the world, feeds on tiny animal plankton. Humans enter the food chain at every link, eating animals from each group and even eating some of the larger seaweeds.

The chain does not end with all organisms being eaten. Many live out their lives and die. Their bodies drift to the ocean floor. There they are attacked by **bacteria**, which cause them to decay and release their minerals back into the water. The minerals are then used by plants once again to produce food.

Wherever they fit in the food chain, sea creatures must be able to get enough food to live. Each creature has its own way of doing this. Each has a body that is well adapted to the food-gathering process. The eating methods of sea creatures may seem strange, but they are effective.

# Filter Feeders

Spray an aerosol—maybe a room deodorant or hair spray—into the air. Notice the tiny droplets of liquid that float where you have sprayed. Thus do plankton float about in the sea.

Imagine the tiny droplets as being everywhere in the air. Imagine they are your only food. How would you collect them? How would you get enough to eat? These are problems faced by many sea creatures.

The filter feeders have found a solution. Their built-in strainers or sieves separate the food from the water. **Bivalves**, herring, barnacles, krill, and the baleen whales are all filter feeders.

## *Bivalves*

The bivalves are soft, headless blobs of creatures hidden inside hard shells. They are the two-shelled animals such as oysters, mussels, clams, and scallops. For them, eating is a matter of waiting for the food to pass by.

*This blue mussel uses sticky mucus on tiny threads hanging in curtain-like flaps to trap food particles in seawater. (Jeff Rotman)*

Each bivalve is a perfectly formed filter pump that pulls in seawater, cleans it of food, and passes it back out. The animal's **gills** serve as filters. These curtainlike flaps hang down between the two shells, just behind the open edges. The tiny threads of the curtain are coated with sticky **mucus** which traps food particles. Thousands of waving, hairlike **cilia** also cover the threads. Their motion draws fresh seawater into the shells. Waving cilia sort the food, pushing the right-sized pieces through tiny grooves to the mouth. Pieces that are too large are pushed away to be washed out of the shell.

For most sea creatures, the gills are the breathing organs. They separate **oxygen** from the water and pass it into the bloodstream. For bivalves, however, gills are used mainly for food gathering. They may also absorb oxygen, but other parts of the bivalve's body do it better.

Bivalves must pump many gallons of water daily to get the food they need. They can clear an aquarium of all pieces of food in a short time. Wherever bivalves live, then, there must be a steady supply of fresh, food-laden seawater.

### *Herring*

Plankton-eating fish, such as the herring, swim through surface waters with their mouths open. Like bivalves, they must filter their food, but unlike bivalves, their gills are designed only for breathing. The pieces of food must be trapped before they reach the gills.

The herring has built-in strainers called **gill rak-**

**ers**. They are attached to the front end of the gills like tiny combs. As seawater passes through from the mouth and out of the gills, plankton collects on the gill rakers and is pushed on down to the fish's stomach.

Eating takes no special effort on the part of the herring. The fish is surrounded by food. The very act of breathing, which requires the drawing in of seawater, carries with it the act of eating.

## Acorn Barnacle

The acorn barnacle is another filter feeder. It reaches out and grabs its food in a strainer formed by its twelve feathery legs. In quick, rhythmical movements, the legs thrust out from a hole in the top of the barnacle's shell, then scoop in, full of food.

If you observe barnacles in shallow water, you can see the feeding movement. Look for barnacles wherever there is seawater and a hard surface. Look on dock pilings, rocks, and seawalls. The white cone-shaped shells are easy to spot because they often mass together in large colonies. Each member of the colony thrusts forth its feathery strainer. It is a fascinating process to watch.

*Massed together in a large colony, acorn barnacles reach out and grab their food with feathery legs that thrust out from the barnacle's shell. (Jeff Rotman)*

### Krill Shrimp

The krill shrimp is another animal that uses its legs as filters. A number of different tiny animals are known by the name of krill, depending on the part of the world they are in. All have several things in common, however. They are the basic food of the huge baleen whales. They feed on the smaller plant plankton, and thus are the single link in the food chain between plants and the baleen whale. And they float through the waters in enormous schools.

The krill shrimp of the cold Antarctic waters are among the largest and most abundant of the krill. These pink, thumb-sized creatures look like cooked shrimp that have been left in their shells. Two black beads of eyes pop from a krill shrimp's pointed head. Threadlike **antennae** stretch out in front. Five rear pairs of legs serve as paddles for swimming. Six forward pairs form a basket for trapping food.

The feeding legs look like long, jointed combs. They reach out in quick bursts to scoop up seawater, then form into a tight basket. The water is forced out between the combs, leaving plant plankton trapped inside. So quickly do the legs open out and fold in that they appear as a blur. Krill are rapid eaters, indeed.

As huge schools of krill feed near the surface of the water, their color gives a pink cast to the sea. To a baleen whale crusing nearby, this is the signal for dinner time.

### Baleen Whales

The baleen whales include the largest creatures in the sea. Yet, they, too, are filter feeders. Instead of teeth, they have a huge fringe of narrow plates hanging down from the upper jaw. These are the filters. They are called **baleen plates**, and they give the whales their name.

Several kinds of baleen whales roam the oceans. Most have several hundred baleen plates in their mouths. The length and width of the baleen plates vary according to the kind of whale. All are wider at the top and taper down to a point, like long, thin teeth. The outside edge is straight. The inside is a coarse, bristly fringe, perfect for trapping food.

It is hard to imagine the size of the blue whale, the largest creature that ever lived. This baleen whale may grow more than 100 feet (30.5 meters) long, as long as two buses placed end to end. The mouth alone may be 20 feet (6.1 meters) long. More than 300 baleen plates line the jaw, each plate over 3 feet (about 1 meter) long. The throat is pleated like an accordion so that it can expand.

To eat, the blue whale swims rapidly around a school of krill, herding it into a tight mass. Then it lunges into the school, mouth open wide. Thousands of gallons of water and krill fill the whale's mouth and expand its throat. The water is forced out through the baleen plates, much as it is forced from the krill's basket of legs. The food is trapped inside.

Humpbacks are baleen whales that have an unusual way of herding their food. They are smaller than the blues, reaching only about fifty feet (fifteen meters) in length. The semitrailer-sized humpback whale circles beneath a school of krill. It blows a net of bubbles that rises around the school. Then the humpback lunges up through the krill, mouth open. So powerful is its lunge that the whale rises straight up out of the water. It sinks back down to strain its food in the same way as the blue whale.

Another baleen, the black right whale, uses a less active method of feeding. The right is only about half the size of the blue, but its baleen plates are longer than most grown men are tall. Since it is not able to

*Lunging up through a school of krill, a powerful humpback whale rises straight up out of Glacier Bay off the coast of Alaska. (John A.K. Davies)*

expand its throat, it skims along the surface of the water with its mouth open. The plankton are caught in the fine fringe of the baleens.

Right whales are noisy eaters. They must shake the baleen plates to remove the plankton before swallowing it. The resulting smacking sound carries long distances over the water. It is easy to tell when a right whale has had a good meal.

As long as enough plankton float in the sea, filter feeders will have plenty of food. Whatever method they use to strain the water, their personal filters work well. Gills, gill rakers, legs, and baleens—these are the eating utensils of the filter feeders.

# 2 Grazers

Seaweed patches and algae-covered rocks and **corals** are pastures for the grazers of the sea. Here, colorful parrotfish, slow-moving snails, squashy sea hares, and prickly sea urchins find their food. They scrape, bite, and grind as they feed on the plants of the sea.

### Parrotfish

Parrotfish are among the largest of the herbivores, or plant eaters. They range from one to six feet (about one-third to two meters) in length and sometimes are much longer. These brilliantly colored fish of the coral reefs get their name from the shape of their teeth. The teeth are fused together into a beaklike shape that juts out from the mouth. It is a shape well adapted for scraping plants from the surfaces of corals and rocks. A set of flat teeth in the throat serves as grinders.

Like most of the grazers, parrotfish are so forceful in their scraping that they nip off bits of coral along

*This brilliantly colored parrotfish has teeth fused together in a beaklike shape, well adapted for scraping plants on corals and rocks. (Jeff Rotman)*

with the plants. A swimmer can learn to recognize the crunching sound of the bony beaks as they scrape away, leaving bite marks wherever they go.

The rainbow parrotfish glistens in reds, blues, and greens as it feeds throughout the day. At night, it does a most peculiar thing. Settling down on the sand, it **secretes** a curtain of mucus, or slime. With this, it builds a private bedchamber around itself, leaving an opening in front for water to flow in and one in back for water to flow out. After a peaceful night's sleep, the parrotfish gets rid of its temporary room and goes back about its job of eating.

### *Periwinkle*

Snails also build their own chambers—their shells. They live in them permanently. The shell is the snail's skeleton, worn on the outside. The soft animal inside creeps along by means of a single foot. The plant-eating snails eat as they creep.

Periwinkles are fingertip-sized snails that live in great numbers on rocky and grassy shores. Some live by scraping away the almost invisible plants that form a slippery film on sea-covered rocks. Others climb stalks of seaweeds and marsh grasses, eating as they go.

These tiny creatures have one thing in common with the huge sharks: a never-ending supply of teeth. But that is the only way these sea animals are alike. The periwinkle's teeth are arranged in rows on a long, ribbonlike tongue called a **radula**. The radula is coiled like the spring of a clock. If stretched straight out, it would be much longer than the snail itself.

*Perched on the shore of Cape Cod, these periwinkles have a neverending supply of teeth arranged in rows on a long, ribbonlike tongue. (Lynn Stone)*

The periwinkle uses its radula like a file, scraping away at plants. So effective is the filing action that bits of rock are also ground away. As the teeth wear down, they are replaced by new teeth. And the periwinkle keeps on eating.

## Limpet

Limpets are some of the best known grazers of the sea world. These rock-dwelling snails are noted for their ability to scrape algae from rock surfaces, leaving clear little paths wherever they have been.

Each limpet selects a permanent home spot on a rock. Its small, round tent-shaped shell fits tightly against the surface. It is held in place by a strong, muscular foot.

At feeding time, the limpet lifts its shell and pulls forward with its foot. A small head with two waving **tentacles** leads the way through a patch of algae. As the limpet moves, its head swings from side to side, scraping up algae with the radula. A two-inch-long (five-centimeter-long) limpet may venture from two to three feet (about two-thirds to one meter) from home. When feeding time is over, the limpet returns to its home and settles in the groove it has worn there.

*The strange-looking sea hare has a shell hidden inside its body. It grazes on seaweeds and has three stomachs to absorb its food. (Lynn Stone)*

### Sea Hare

Patches of seaweed often shelter the grazing sea hare. This strange-looking creature is a snail that has its shell hidden inside its body.

If lifted from the water, the sea hare is a shapeless, slimy blob. In its watery home, it has a strange but definite shape. Some people think it looks like a hunched-up rabbit or hare. It has two sets of fleshy tentacles, one set on the front of its head and one set farther back. The back set sticks up like the ears of a hare.

The sea hare grazes on the large seaweeds, using its radula to file off pieces. Three stomachs are waiting for the food. The first is merely a passage to the second, which is lined with teeth. Here the weeds are ground into smaller bits and passed on to the third stomach, which has more grinding teeth.

Sea hares may be as large as or larger than land hares or rabbits, but they are often hard to see. Their colors blend with the sea bottom and with the seaweeds that are their food. If disturbed, they give off a purple fluid.

### Sea Urchin

Seaweed patches harbor another grazer—the sea urchin. This creature looks somewhat like a pincushion with the points of colorful pins pointing outward. The body is a rounded, hard skeleton covered with pinlike spines. Many long, thin **tube feet** stretch out almost invisibly from among the spines.

The mouth is on the underside, hidden from view as the urchin makes its slow way across the sand or

*Spiny sea urchins use their sharp teeth to scrape algae from rocks or chew through large strands of seaweed. (Jeff Rotman)*

rock. Five shining white teeth surround the mouth. These scrape algae from rocks or chew through large strands of seaweed.

Some urchins burrow in the sand or even in soft rock. They use their spines and teeth to scrape away the hard surfaces. Their tube feet help gather food, bringing it in to the mouth. Some urchins eat meat, but most make plants the major part of their diet.

Like the filter feeders that feed on plant plankton, the grazers are part of the first animal link in the food chain. Large or small, they must have a steady supply of plants on which to feed. And large or small, they in turn become food for meat eaters.

 *Gulpers*

Filter feeders eat the tiny, floating life of the sea, and gulpers eat the filter feeders. At least, they eat the filter feeders that are small enough to swallow whole. Most fish are gulpers.

### Bluefin Tuna

The bluefin tuna is typical of gulpers that need only a big mouth to match a big appetite. A tuna as large as a big man will have a bucket-sized mouth. Its tiny teeth are of little use because the tuna sucks in its fish dinner with a mouthful of water. Most of the water goes out the gills. The fish go into the tuna's stomach.

The tuna has a body built for speed. With rapid beats of its strong tail, the tuna takes off in a silvery blue flash. It can reach fifty-five miles (eighty-eight kilometers) an hour in short bursts. Smaller fish do not stand a chance when sighted by a hungry tuna.

Schools of tuna cruise the sea looking for schools

Large tuna, such as the yellowfin tuna shown here, have bucket-sized mouths that suck in smaller fish with mouthfuls of water.

of food fish. When the two meet, the water becomes a churning mass of activity. Excited tuna charge into the food fish, mouths open wide. Twisting, turning, even leaping into the air, the tuna gulp until gorged.

### Cod

While tuna feed in open waters, cod do most of their gulping along the sea bottom. Cod are smaller than tuna. They are about two to three feet (about two-thirds to one meter) long. But cod are no less hungry. In fact, they are such greedy creatures that they gulp whatever they can find that looks like food.

Generally, cod eat small fish, shrimp, crabs, and shellfish. The cod has no problem getting food that is hidden in shells. It just swallows its victims whole. Strong **acids** in the cod's stomach dissolve the shells as well as the meat inside.

There are times, though, when the cods' gulps bring in strange objects. People fishing have found keys, cans, and even a book in cods' stomachs.

### Black Swallower

When it comes to gulping, it is hard to beat the black swallower. This little six-inch (fifteen-centimeter) fish can swallow a fish twice its size.

Food is scarce in the cold, dark part of the deep sea where the black swallower lives. It must take what food it can get, and it must make it last a long time.

The body of the black swallower is built for over-eating. A wide mouth and needle-sharp teeth grab the swallower's food. Movable teeth in its throat help push the food down. To get food to its stomach, the swallower must move its head and gills out of the way. Then its stomach stretches to hold the huge meal. The little fish bobs along on top of its full, balloon-shaped belly.

There are many gulpers in the sea. The tuna, cod, and black swallower are typical. Whatever their food, they suck it in with a gulp of water and swallow it whole. Gulpers use their teeth only to seize and hold their slippery dinner so that it doesn't get away.

# ④ *Biters and Slashers*

Biters and slashers are meat eaters. Like the gulpers, they eat the filter feeders. Some even eat the gulpers.

Biters and slashers include some of the most savage creatures in the sea—the sharks, barracudas, and killer whales. They also include the sawfish, the swordfish, and the many-armed squid and octopuses.

If the food to be eaten is larger than the eater, biting is a good way to get it down to size. Biters and slashers need strong, sharp teeth or beaks. These are the eating utensils that tear and shred food into bite-sized pieces for swallowing.

### Barracuda

Barracudas and sharks are the terrors of the sea. They attack their food, biting savagely. Size is no protection from these **predators**. They do not hesitate to attack animals larger than themselves. They will even attack humans.

The barracuda has a mouth full of razor-sharp

*Barracudas are predators that have mouths full of razor-sharp teeth and attack large fish with lightning-fast speed. (Jeff Rotman)*

teeth. It attacks with lightning-fast speed. In a single, swift strike, it can bite a large fish in two.

Hunting alone, the barracuda will follow a school of fish, like a tiger stalking its prey. It will even herd fish, keeping them huddled together in fear. That way the barracuda can keep dinner nearby until it is ready to eat.

### Great White Shark

The great white shark is a power-packed bundle of fury when it is hungry. Streamlined and strong, it lunges upward from beneath its **prey**. Its open jaws are filled with several rows of knifelike teeth. Clamping down on its prey, the great white shakes powerfully from side to side. It tears off a huge, bite-sized chunk, then lunges back for more.

Great whites may grow more than 20 feet (6.1 meters) long and have been known to reach 30 feet (9.1 meters). Their huge jaws can completely surround a person. Nowhere is there a more fearsome looking fish.

In the force of their attacks, sharks and barracudas lose many teeth. For them the loss is not important since they have a lifetime supply of new ones waiting to fill any gaps. The savages of the sea are well equipped for biting.

Not all sharks, though, are as ferocious as the great white. In fact, an even larger shark, the whale shark, is a filter feeder.

### Cookie Cutter Shark

A small, foot-long shark has earned the name cookie cutter for its unusual method of eating. Its round little mouth and small size do not keep it from attacking large fish. But it can scarcely do much damage to a big tuna. It merely bites out a round, cookie-shaped chunk, and then swims on. The victim is probably not even aware something is missing. The wound soon heals. Meanwhile, the cookie cutter goes from fish to fish, helping itself to a bite here and a bite there.

### Killer Whale

The killer whale is the most beautiful of the biters. This graceful black-and-white creature is a star performer at several public **seaquariums**. In such huge, seawater-filled tanks, the killer whale appears to get enough to eat from a handfed diet of small fish.

In the open sea, however, food is not always so easily available.

In the wild, the killer whale must attack to live. It will eat almost anything that swims in the sea. Fish, seals, seabirds, and dolphins are normal meals. Even the huge blue whale may be attacked and killed by packs of killer whales.

The powerful tail fins, or **flukes**, of the killer whale aid in food gathering. When attacking a seal or sea lion, the killer flips the unlucky creature with its tail. Though the victim weighs several hundred pounds, it flies into the air like a tennis ball. Twenty or thirty feet up it goes before falling back into the sea. Then the killer flips it again. The stunned prey cannot fight or flee. It soon becomes a meal for the whale.

### Sawfish

The sawfish can also stun its prey before eating it. Its top jaw extends into a broad, flat saw, one-half as long as the rest of its body. Sharp teeth line each side of the saw. Charging into a school of fish, the sawfish slashes back and forth with its saw. Some fish are killed outright, while others are merely stunned. Either way, they are soon eaten.

*The sawfish's top jaw extends into a broad, flat saw that it uses as a weapon to slash through a school of fish. (Jeff Rotman)*

### Swordfish

Like the sawfish, the swordfish has its own special weapon for slashing and stunning food. Its top jaw, or front end, is a double-edged sword. From the point of its sword to the tip of its tail, the swordfish may be 11 feet (3.3 meters) long. Even larger ones have been known. The sword is about one-third of the total length.

Coming up from below a school of fish, the swordfish slashes like the sawfish. The charge of a swordfish is so powerful that the sword can pierce the wooden beams or planks of a ship. Fish are no match for such a weapon.

### Squid

Biters and slashers usually have large appetites. The many-armed squid is no exception. Although its mouth is small compared to the mouths of biting fish and whales, it is just as forceful in its eating habits.

The squid's mouth is a beak, shaped much like that of a parrot. The beak is surrounded by eight long arms and two even longer tentacles. Two bulging eyes mark the rest of the head. The body tapers out behind, its filmy fins fluttering in the current. A squid may be

*The squid's mouth is a beak surrounded by eight long arms and two even longer tentacles. Here you can see one of the squid's two bulging eyes. (Jeff Rotman)*

smaller than your thumb or as long as a five-story building is tall.

The creature moves rapidly—backward, forward, or sideways. This is a definite advantage when it comes to catching food. After shooting backward into a school of fish, a squid will suddenly dart to one side and seize a fish with its tentacles. A quick bite on the neck kills the fish. Then, off goes its head, and the rest of the fish becomes bite-sized chunks.

Since a squid's beak is strong enough to cut a heavy wire in two, the shells of crabs and lobsters pose no problems. These creatures, as well as fish, must beware of hungry squids.

One major enemy of the squid sometimes becomes its victim. The large-toothed whales, such as the killer whale, dive deep into the ocean to find the huge squid that live hidden there. Sometimes, though, the squid is bigger or smarter than the whale. Long arms covered with suckers grab the whale and hang on. The sharp squid beak attacks the tough skin of the whale. If lucky, the whale is able to bite off a squid arm or two and escape with its life. The squid then settles down to **regenerate**, or regrow, its arm.

### Octopus

The octopus is also a biter with a beak and long arms. Its eight arms are covered with suckers, similar to those of the squid. Its body, though, is more rounded and has no fins. From arm tip to arm tip, an octopus may measure from two inches (five centimeters) to thirty-two feet (nearly ten meters) across.

The octopus uses its arms to pull unsuspecting

*The octopus uses its eight arms to catch snails, clams, crabs, lobsters, and even fish. (Jeff Rotman)*

snails off rocks or pilings. It may also collect an arm-load of clams from the sea floor, passing the shellfish from sucker to sucker up its arms. The shellfish are taken back to the octopus's cave to be eaten when it is hungry.

For a quick, on-the-spot meal, the octopus traps a crab or lobster with its arms. It bites a hole in the shell, injects a poison and a digestive juice, and then eats its prey. Fish, too, are caught in the web of the arms and attacked by the beak.

The biters and slashers are powerful eaters. They know how to attack their food. Like all creatures, they must eat to live. Attacking and biting are their keys to survival.

# 5 Drillers and Hammerers

The hard shells of bivalves provide little protection from two groups of animals—the drillers and the hammerers. Like miniature carpenters, moon snails and oyster drills use built-in drills to bore through shells. Knobbed whelks and sea otters use their hammering skills to break open the shells that hide their favorite foods.

### Moon Snail

If you search the seashore for shells, you are likely to find one, especially a bivalve, with a little round hole near the top of the shell. It will look almost as if someone had drilled the hole just so the shell could be threaded on a chain and worn as a necklace.

The hole was, indeed, drilled—but not by a person. A little snail was responsible for the job. Its purpose was to get food, not to provide you with a necklace.

The moon snail is a clam hunter. It has no eyes,

*A moon snail makes a meal of a lobster claw. In search of food, it plows through the dark areas beneath the sandy sea bottom. (Lynn Stone)*

and needs none, since it spends its time plowing through the dark areas beneath the sandy sea bottom. With a foot three times as long as its shell, it reaches out in search of a clam. Even clams buried under a foot of sand are not safe from a hungry moon snail.

When grabbed firmly by the moon snail's foot, a clam cannot move. Out comes the snail's radula, through its long, tubelike **proboscis**, or snout. The radula files a tiny hole through the hard outer layer of the clam's shell. Drops of acid secreted by a boring gland may help finish the job. Once through the shell, the radula scrapes the soft clam meat into bits and passes them up the proboscis. Stomach teeth grind the food into even smaller bits.

A hungry moon snail will even attack others of its own kind. With its huge foot, it can smother another snail by covering its opening. It may wait for the snail to die, or it may begin boring right away as it does with clams.

### Oyster Drill

The oyster drill eats all kinds of bivalves, but it is particularly fond of young oysters with thin shells. A group of these carnivorous, or meat-eating, snails can do much damage to an oyster bed. Each snail may kill as many as 200 oysters in a season.

When the oyster drill settles down for a meal, it does not hurry. First the oyster drill selects a likely bivalve and sits on it. Then out comes its radula, and the drilling begins. The process is aided by drops of acid secreted by a gland in the bottom of the snail's foot. This helps soften the shell.

It may take two or more days for the snail to bore through a shell. The snail has plenty of time. Its victim is not going anywhere. Oysters, for example, are stuck in one place for life and have only their shells for protection.

Once the hole is complete, the snail sticks its proboscis in and helps itself to dinner. When the oyster dies, its shells open. Other meat eaters—crabs, fish, and other snails—soon join the oyster drills. If left to itself, the drill will spend almost a full day and night on its meal. If there are too many guests, however, it soon moves on and finds another victim.

### Knobbed Whelk

The large knobbed whelks do not bother to drill for their food. They, too, attack bivalves. But they

*Knobbed whelks pry or hammer at the shells of bivalves until they have an opening large enough to slip in a proboscis and eat the soft meat inside. (Lynn Stone)*

either pry or hammer at the shells until they have an opening large enough to slip a proboscis into.

The whelk slips across the sandy bottom on its large, flat, muscular foot. It depends on its sense of smell to locate bivalves buried in the sand or resting on the bottom. Like the moon snail, the whelk grips the shell with its foot. It pulls mightily on the top shell and uses the lip of its own shell to pry open the valves.

*The sea otter brings food to the surface and eats floating on its back.*

If this method doesn't work, then the hammering begins.

By using its muscles, the whelk lifts its own shell and pounds it against the edges of the bivalve's shells. The whelk's shell is large enough and heavy enough that it soon chips away an opening. In goes the proboscis, and out comes dinner.

### Sea Otter

Since the sea otter has no shell of its own, it selects a rock to serve as its hammer. It is one of the few animals to use a tool.

The sea otter is a delightfully playful creature. Its glossy dark-brown-to-black fur glistens as it skims through the waters near rocky shores. It dives down for food, gathering crabs, sea urchins, and shellfish in its forepaws. It may use its teeth to catch fish and octopuses.

Food is brought to the surface, where the otter can eat as it floats on its back. Its chest serves as a table. When a shellfish is on the menu, the otter brings up a flat stone along with the shellfish. Laying the rock on its chest, the otter smashes the shellfish against it, hammering down again and again until the shell breaks. The stone is also used to hammer abalone shells away from rocks where they are stuck fast.

Such use of a tool is unusual for animals. But to a hungry otter, it is a natural way of getting to the soft meat hidden inside hard shells. The softer shells of crabs and sea urchins are easily crushed by the otter's broad, flat teeth. For that food, no tool is needed.

Drilling and hammering may seem like hard ways to get one's food. But for the drillers and hammerers, it works. For them, that is what is most important.

 # 6 Fishers

If you wanted to catch a fish, you would probably take a pole, a line, and some kind of bait or lure and go fishing. That it what an angler fish does every day. Its fishing pole is always with it, built into the angler's body. Worm snails, archerfish, and dipper clams are also fishers. Their methods are different than yours or the angler fish's, but they work just as well.

## Goosefish

The most common angler fish in American waters is the goosefish. A similar species prefers European waters. Neither is appreciated by human anglers.

The broad, flat, bulky goosefish lies on the sea bottom. Unless you looked carefully, you would think the goosefish was no more than a seaweed-covered rock. Its speckled brown color blends with the sand. Little strings of flesh, called barbels, dangle from its chin and the sides of its body. The whole front of its broad head opens into an enormous mouth. Inside, the

*The goosefish waits patiently while its fishing rod—a spine and flap of skin sticking out of its head—dangles just above its mouth. (Jeff Rotman)*

four rows of teeth are sharply pointed.

The goosefish appears to be slow and sluggish. Actually, it is waiting patiently, like any good angler. Its fishing rod is a spine sticking out of the top of its head. A fleshy flap of skin dangles from the end like bait. Slowly, the fish moves its rod back and forth, the bait dangling just above its mouth. Any fish that tries to bite has a big surprise coming. Like a flash, the seemingly lazy goosefish opens its mouth and seizes the helpless creature in its teeth. Then, with one gulp, the fish is swallowed.

The size of the goosefish's appetite matches the size of its mouth. It can swallow a fish almost as large as itself. And it does not stop with just one. A full-grown goosefish can be more than 4 feet (1.2 meters) long and can weigh more than 50 pounds (22.7 kilograms). It varies its diet by swimming to the surface and gulping down unsuspecting seabirds floating there. One human angler caught a goosefish with seven ducks in its stomach.

### Worm Snail

Worm snails are also fishers. They spin their own fishing line from a special gland in their single foot.

The young worm snail starts out looking like most other snails. Its single shell spirals from a point, getting larger toward the open end. As the snail grows, however, the open end of its shell soon stops spiraling. Instead, it grows into a long tube that curves around in various directions. Its wormlike shape gives the snail its name.

The five-inch-long (thirteen-centimeter-long)

snail throws out fishing lines more than twice its own length. Each line is covered with a sticky mucus. Soon, many plankton animals are trapped in the mucus, unable to wriggle away. The worm snail then draws in its lines and has a feast.

### Dipper Clam

Another seashell, the dipper clam, has developed an effective method of fishing. Unlike the filter-feeding clams, it has no gills, no mucus, and no cilia. Without them, it cannot strain plankton from the seawater. Instead, it traps its food.

The shape of the dipper's shells gives the clam its name. The dipper has two round, flat shells that fit together like those of any other clam. On one edge, however, they taper out into what looks like a short spoon handle. Not much could be dipped with it, though, since the entire shell is only about half as long as a person's thumb.

Dippers lie buried in the sand or mud of deep waters. Two **siphons**, or tubes, stretch up from their tapered end. One is equipped with a valve, or trap door. As the clam pumps water into the siphon, tiny animals are drawn in. As the water passes through and out the second siphon, the animals are trapped by the valve. Muscular flaps push them into the mouth, and the dipper has its meal.

### Archerfish

The strangest of all the fishers is the archerfish. It shoots its food.

Whenever the archerfish sees a likely-looking insect near the water's edge, it spits a series of tiny drops of water. The force of the drops is great enough to knock an insect off a leaf three feet (about one meter) away. When the victim falls into the water, the fish has a meal.

The archerfish lives in Asian waters. It likes freshwater streams and the slightly salty waters of **estuaries** on the edge of the sea.

The eight-inch-long (twenty-centimeter-long) fish prowls the water's edge searching for insects. Its vision must be good, since it spots the insects from underwater. Its aim is excellent, too, as many an unsuspecting insect has discovered.

Fishers of the sea are skilled at what they do. They have to be. Their lives depend on their catches.

# 7 Farmers

Two kinds of sea creatures take no chances on finding enough food. They raise their own. A clam and a fish are the farmers. They have their own special methods of raising their crops.

### Giant Clam

The giant clam is often called a "man-eating clam." The largest of all bivalves, it has shells more than three feet (about one meter) across. The two shells together may weigh 500 pounds (227 kilograms). The clam is big enough and strong enough to catch a diver's foot or arm between its shells. Whether it ever does is doubtful. Certainly it would not actually eat a person. It is a plant eater, like most other clams, and thrives on plankton and its own crop of algae.

The clam's garden plot is the soft tissue on the edges of its **mantle**. The mantle is an envelope of skin that enfolds the body of the clam. The open edges hang over the edges of the shell. All clams have man-

tles, but that of the giant clam is unusually colorful. Its purple fringes are marked with green.

Crops of brown-colored algae are grown in the flesh of the mantle edges. Here the crops are exposed to the sunlight that filters through the shallow waters above the clam. Clear cells in the clam's skin operate like magnifying glasses. They concentrate the sunlight so that it reaches deep into the areas that might not otherwise receive enough light. The minerals, or fertilizer, needed by the algae are supplied from the clam's own wastes.

The giant clam's garden supplies much of its food. Blood cells carry the algae straight into its digestive system. Other food is obtained in the usual way of clams. It is filtered from the seawater by the gills. The giant clam should never go hungry, in spite of its huge size.

### Three-spot Damselfish

Another sea farmer is a four-inch-long (ten-centimeter-long) black-and-gray fish, the three-spot damselfish. It lives among the corals in a reef. It is on the coral itself that the damselfish raises its crop of algae.

*The giant clam, the largest of all bivalves, grows its own algae in the soft tissue on the edges of its mantle. (Jeff Rotman)*

The damselfish prepares its garden by biting off the polyps of staghorn corals. In this way it kills a wide area of the coral, leaving only the exposed skeletons. Soon algae, growing quickly in the sunlit tropical waters, cover the bare coral stalks.

Once its garden has started to grow, the damselfish guards it from all strangers. It does not hesitate to attack any invader, including a diver. For the damselfish, its garden is worth fighting for. The garden is not only the fish's major source of food, but it is also a nesting site.

Many damselfish may farm on a large area of coral. Working together on such a farm is good for the fish themselves. However, it destroys the coral.

Farming in the sea is an unusual way for sea creatures to get their food. For the giant clam and the three-spot damselfish, it is a way that works well.

*The damselfish prepares its garden of algae by biting off the polyps of corals, allowing the algae to cover the bare coral stalks. (Charles Arneson)*

# 8 Shockers

Shockers generate electricity in their bodies and use it to stun their prey. They also use it to defend themselves and possibly to help find their way in murky waters.

Of all the animals, only fish are able to produce electricity. This unusual ability is limited to a very few kinds of fish. Several live in fresh water. The electric rays and the stargazers are the shockers of the sea.

### Electric Ray

The electric ray does not look like a typical fish. Its head and upper body are flattened into a broad, round disk. The soft, flexible sides of the disk flap like wings to carry the fish gracefully through the water. Two eyes stare from the top of the head. A small mouth is hidden underneath. The ray may reach 5 feet (1.5 meters) in both length and width.

Also known as the torpedo or numbfish, the elec-

*The torpedo ray uses electric organs in its wing flaps to stun fish with 220 volts of electric force. (Jeff Rotman)*

tric ray lives in shallow waters. It prefers the warm or moderate temperatures off the coasts of North America and Europe.

The electric ray's organs are in the wing flaps. Carrying a jolt of 220 **volts**, they are powerful enough to knock a person down. Against such an electric force, small fish do not stand a chance. The ray simply wraps a fish in its wing, stuns it, and has its meal.

### *Stargazer*

The electric charge of the stargazer is much milder than that of the ray. The stargazer's electric organs are located in pits behind its eyes. They can generate fifty volts of electricity, enough to stun a small animal.

The stargazer is a bottom fish. It lies buried in the sand with only its head exposed. Its eyes are high on its head, and they look straight up, as if gazing at the stars. The stargazer's mouth opens upward, just in front of its eyes. It is ready to grab any passing fish or crab. As the creature's mouth opens, an electric shock probably stuns its prey.

The stargazer is definitely a fish to avoid. This foot-long, plump little creature not only packs an electric charge, but has poisonous spines as well.

What makes a fish electric? That is a question of interest to scientists. People create very small electrical impulses whenever they use a muscle. In this way human nerves give messages to the muscles to make them respond. In the electric fish, the muscle response has become weakened and the electrical response greatly strengthened.

Special cells called **electroplates** serve as batteries to store the electricity in the fish. They are attached in a series, just as the batteries in a flashlight. A large ray may have more than a thousand electroplates. When they all release their power at once, the result is a stunning shock.

# 9 Poisoners

When its food has a habit of swimming away, a predator needs some way to stop it. Some sea animals solve the problem with poison. Stinging cells or **venom sacs** supply the amount of poison needed to **paralyze** the prey.

Cone snails, scorpionfish, and the jellylike animals are all poisoners. Some can even be dangerous to people. At the least, they can cause a painful sting. Their poison, though, is mostly intended to help gather food. It also serves to protect them from enemies—and to these creatures, a person is an enemy.

### Cone Snail

The beautiful shells of the cone snails give no sign of the danger hidden within. Colorful designs mark the cone-shaped shells. The snail extends its broad, flat foot from the long, narrow opening of its shell. Its head sticks out from one end, its tentacles leading the way for the foot and shell. The large proboscis hides

*The cone snail reaches out to its prey with its long proboscis, and injects poison with its needle-thin, arrow-shaped teeth. (Charles Arneson)*

the radula and the poison tube. Inside, a supply of needle-thin, arrow-shaped teeth is stored and ready for use.

When the cone snail finds a worm, a small fish, or another snail to eat, it goes into action. The proboscis reaches out to its prey. An arrow-tooth shoots into its skin, injecting poison. Then the cone pulls both tooth and prey into its mouth and swallows them.

Some cones in the South Pacific have poison as powerful as that of a rattlesnake. One of these snails is the beautiful textile cone of the Hawaiian Islands. People have died as a result of its bite.

Many different species of cones are found in warm waters throughout the world. Most have not harmed people. However, just to be safe, any large cone should be handled with care.

### Scorpionfish

Scorpionfish are a group of poison-packed fish. They are sometimes known as rockfish or stonefish. Many different species inhabit the world's seas. Their plump bodies are mottled with color and covered by numerous fins, spines, and fleshy tabs. The spines carry the poison.

The lionfish is one of the scorpionfish. It hides its black-and-yellow body in the sand, lying in wait for passing fish. Sharp spines on its back act like **hypodermic** needles. A tiny sac on each spine holds the paralyzing **venom**. One shot is enough to capture any small creature that makes the mistake of passing by. Like scorpions on land, scorpionfish in the sea are creatures to avoid.

*The sharp spines on the back of the lionfish shoot paralyzing venom into any small creature that passes nearby. (Charles Arneson)*

### Jelly Animals

Jellyfish and their many relatives are also poisoners. The floating Portuguese man-of-war, the flowerlike sea anemone, and the reef-building coral are all part of this family. All are blind. None have brains. Yet, like all creatures, the jelly animals are experts at gathering food.

The jellys are carnivorous. They thrive on creatures such as small fish, worms, and animal plankton. Their food-gathering tools are tentacles equipped with stinging cells called **nematocysts**. Each nematocyst is a tiny poison-filled capsule with a long, coiled thread inside. When touched, the thread shoots out and pierces the toucher. A paralyzing poison is injected. Then tentacles carry the prey to the jelly's mouth.

Each tentacle has many nematocysts. Since each can be used only once, new nematocysts are constantly being produced. The jellys are active poison factories.

The bodies of the various jelly animals feel somewhat like gelatin. They are 98 percent water and are often delicate and flowerlike. Some are tiny, like the coral polyps hidden inside their rocklike homes.

Others, like some of the free-floating jellyfish, are huge. All have simple, saclike bodies, open at one end and closed at the other. The open end is the mouth, which is surrounded by tentacles. The closed end is equipped either for attaching or for floating.

### Jellyfish

The major floaters are the jellyfish themselves. Their umbrella-shaped bodies open and close slowly and rhythmically. This movement creates a current of water that gently moves the creatures by a kind of jet propulsion, or power.

The jellyfish's tentacles hang down from the umbrella, ready to trap and sting passing fish. A person coming in contact with the tentacles would also be stung. How badly would depend on the kind of jellyfish. The little moon jellyfish that often washes ashore after a storm might cause an itching rash. The largest jellyfish in the world, however, could cause severe burning and blistering. This is the Lion's Mane, or red jelly, which reaches a size of eight feet (about two and a half meters) across. Its 150 tentacles can trap a large fish. Fortunately, it is seldom found near shore.

### Portuguese Man-of-War

Another floater to watch out for is the Portuguese man-of-war. Its pale blue balloons float on the surface of the sea. Underneath hang some of the longest and most deadly tentacles in the world. When fully extended, the tentacles beneath a foot-wide man-of-war balloon can reach 100 feet (30.5 meters) beneath the surface. They spread out like a net to trap and kill fish. The blue, beadlike nematocysts contain some of the sea's deadliest poison. Even a dead man-of-war's stingers can cause severe burns and blisters.

### Anemones

Unlike the floating jellies, anemones are attached to something. It may be a rock, a piling, or a shell. It may be the sea bottom itself.

Instead of hanging down, the tentacles of anemones reach up into the water. The animal itself is merely a double-walled tube, closed at the bottom. The open end, or mouth, is surrounded by short, fleshy tentacles. They wave about in the water, forming colorful patterns and designs.

Sea anemones are called the "flowers of the sea" because of their delicate beauty. Their tentacles open

*The Lion's Mane, or red jelly, is the largest jellyfish in the world. Its 150 tentacles can trap a large fish. (Jeff Rotman)*

out like the petals of a flower. When closed, they form a jellylike blob.

Each species of anemone has its own pattern of petals. The common frilled anemone has as many as 1,000 tentacles bunched in semicircles to form a frilled flower. Their colors may be white, reddish brown, yellowish, or similar shades.

Despite their flowerlike beauty, anemones are animals. Like all animals, they must eat. The delicate tentacle petals are covered with nematocysts, just as those of the jellyfish.

Any tiny animal that ventures too close to an anemone is in immediate danger. An arrowhead of poison explodes from the nematocyst. Tentacles curl around the paralyzed animal, and into the anemone's mouth it goes.

### Coral Polyps

Coral polyps are much like anemones, except they are hidden inside hard skeletons. Each polyp builds its own stony cup, using lime from seawater.

Millions of stony corals bunch together to form huge reefs. As older corals die, young ones settle onto their skeletons. Within the reef, there are different

*The common frilled anemone has as many as 1,000 tentacles. Its delicate tentacle petals are covered with nematocysts filled with poison. (Jeff Rotman)*

*A close-up view of the poisonous tentacles of a coral polyp.*

kinds of corals. Each kind forms colonies of a different shape. There are staghorn, brain, and star corals, among others. What do the names say about their shapes?

At feeding time, the reef is alive with the colorful tentacles of coral polyps. Each tiny animal reaches out from the safety of its stony cup. Poisonous tentacles gather microscopic animals from surrounding seawater.

Some corals even eat each other. Long, thin threads inside the animal help digest its food. These same threads can be extended out of the body. When they touch a polyp of a different species, they simply digest it. No trip to the mouth is needed.

Poisoners are effective food gatherers. As long as enough food passes within reach of their poison organs, they are satisfied.

# 10 Guests —Friendly and Unfriendly

Some sea creatures find their meals as a result of being another's guest. Sometimes this relationship works out happily for both, as with the cleaner wrasses and the man-of-war fish. In the case of the sea lamprey, however, the host fish would prefer to do without its unwelcome guest.

### Sea Lamprey

The sea lamprey is a **parasite**, an animal that lives on the body of another and at the other's expense. Like the fleas on a dog, the lamprey feeds on the blood of its host. Unlike the flea, though, it is big—as long as three feet (about one meter). And it latches on with a grip of death.

The whole front of the lamprey's head is a jawless round mouth, shaped like a suction cup. More than 100 sharp teeth fill the inside of the cup. A rough tongue in the middle has more teeth on its surface.

If you open your mouth into a circle, then place it

against your hand and suck, you will get some idea of how the lamprey attaches to the host fish. The lamprey's hold is much tighter than yours, however, since the lamprey's lip is one nonstop circle around its mouth. The lip's fringed edge forms a tight seal.

The rasping tongue and teeth go to work until the host fish's scales and skin are pierced. From then on, the lamprey has a steady food supply. At least, it is steady until the fish dies, and the lamprey moves on to another victim.

Lampreys do much damage to the supply of some fish that people catch for food. The problems fleas cause a dog are minor compared to those a lamprey causes its host.

### Cleaner Wrasse

Other parasites that bother fish are much smaller than the lamprey. Tiny fish lice attach to the gills, mouth, and skin of some fish. Though not as deadly as the lamprey, they are uncomfortable and a nuisance. In large numbers, they can drain the energy of even the largest fish. Tiny parasites such as this offer a welcome treat to another kind of sea guest—the cleaner fish.

*A cleaner wrasse cleans parasites off the gills of a larger fish in the colorful waters of the Red Sea. (Jeff Rotman)*

The colorful little cleaner wrasse is a fish that makes its living cleaning parasites, dead skin, and bacteria from larger fish. Its pointed snout and tweezerlike teeth are perfectly designed to pick and nibble.

In tropical waters, the cleaner wrasse sets up shop in one particular spot each day. Its customers know where to come for service, and come they do. From far out in the ocean, large fish come to get cleaning service. A cleaning station can often be identified by the group of fish waiting patiently to be served.

Cleaner wrasses are usually easy to spot. A broad stripe marks the body from head to tail. Then, just to be sure there is no mistake, the cleaner performs a little water dance. A special wriggling motion of its body signals that the cleaner is ready to service the larger fish.

Customer fish float almost motionless while the cleaner works. If the cleaner gives a little nudge, the customer lifts its gills, opens its mouth, or bares its teeth. The cleaner works up and down the fish's body, over its eyes, and even into its mouth to pick away unwanted mites.

Normally the four-inch (ten-centimeter) cleaner would be a perfect snack for the large fish it cleans. In tropical waters, it is safe. It performs its job and receives food and protection in return. The customer fish looks elsewhere for its meal. The cleaner is too valuable an ally to be eaten.

Cleaners in cooler waters are not always so fortunate. There the host fish may decide to make a meal of its helpful guest, but only after the host has been carefully cleaned.

### False Cleaner Fish

The false cleaner fish looks very much like the cleaner wrasse. It performs the same little wriggling dance to identify itself to a host fish. The false cleaner is not interested in parasites, though. It wants a bite of the host itself. And get a bite it does!

The unsuspecting host fish allows the false cleaner to approach since the host expects to receive cleaning service. The false cleaner takes advantage of the situation and helps itself to a chunk of fish. It is an unwelcome guest, indeed!

### Man-of-War Fish

The deadly Portuguese man-of-war would hardly seem a likely host for any type of guest. Its poisonous tentacles are something to avoid. Yet, swimming freely among the poison-laden strands lives a small fish—the man-of-war fish.

The speckled, three-inch-long (eight-centimeter-long) fish appears to suffer no ill effects from the poison. Sheltered safely from larger fish that might eat it, the guest fish steals bits of the Portuguese man-of-war's food. In return, it probably helps lure other fish into the man-of-war's tentacle net. When

that happens, both the Portuguese man-of-war and its guest eat well.

The guests of the sea have found their own ways to assure a plentiful food supply. These creatures cannot survive alone. They must have a relationship, either friendly or unfriendly, with other creatures of the sea.

*Swimming among the deadly tentacles of the Portuguese man-of-war, the man-of-war fish eats bits of the larger creature's food. (Charles Arneson)*

# Pinchers and Crawlers

Along the bottom of the sea, many creatures make their way, eating as they crawl. The crabs and lobsters are fitted with **claws** that serve as their eating utensils. The horseshoe crab has legs that both walk and chew. And the sea star lets its stomach do the work. All are meat eaters, though some occasionally add seaweed to their diets.

### Stone Crab

Imagine how hard you could pinch if your bones were on the outside of your hands instead of on the inside. The stone crab's skeleton is on the outside of its body. Its **pincer** claws can crush a whelk shell, and its claw tips can cut like a knife.

In spite of its name, the stone crab is a creature of the sand and mud near shores. It may lie in wait in a dark hole, watching for a whelk or other creature to wander by. It may move across the sand on its eight hairy, jointed legs, searching for a juicy clam or even a dead fish. Its claws will test anything, crushing or tearing, to see if it is good to eat.

Though its claws look awkward, the stone crab uses them with the greatest of ease. Delicate bits of meat are pinched off and carried to the mouth, each piece held as easily as if by a finger and a thumb.

The crab's lipless mouth is made up of a number of hard little segments, or jaw pieces. These open and close rapidly, acting like teeth to crush and tear the food and push it on its way.

The stone crab needs its claws in order to eat. If it loses one, it soon grows another.

### American Lobster

The American lobster has a set of claws that make those of the stone crab look small. As the lobster's body grows, so do its claws, but at a faster rate. By the time a lobster has reached two feet or more in length, its two claws may make up over half its weight. What a lobster dinner that would make!

For the lobster, pincers serve as a built-in knife and fork. One claw has a pincer that is heavy and strongly hooked for grasping and crushing. It is used to hold food and to crack the shells of snails and

bivalves. The pincer on the other claw is thinner and sharper. It is a cutter, tearing meat or plants into small bits.

The lobster's mouth is much like the crab's. It is ready to go to work as soon as it receives the cut-up bits of food.

### Horseshoe Crab

The dome-shaped horseshoe crab has a mouth that is hidden under its body, right in the middle of its five pairs of legs. This arrangement works well for the horseshoe, since its legs do the chewing.

A flat pad at the base of each leg is covered with sharp spines that serve as teeth. As the horseshoe walks, the pads grind. If the horseshoe stands still, it cannot chew—it must walk to eat.

The horseshoe plods across the sea bottom with only its dome-shaped shell and long, pointed tail visible. The pincer-tipped legs are busy underneath, searching out worms and small bivalves for food. As eating utensils, the legs are unusual—pincers at one end and teeth at the other. Since the legs bend easily at several joints, moving food from one end to the other and on into the mouth is no problem. At least it's no

*The American lobster uses its large set of claws to hold and cut food and to crack the shells of snails and bivalves. (Jeff Rotman)*

problem as long as the horseshoe keeps walking. A sit-down dinner is not for this creature of the sea.

### Sea Star

The sea star, on the other hand, makes a habit of sitting on its dinner. Its mouth, like the horseshoe's, is hidden on the underside of its body. But there is no shell to cover the legs, which are what give the sea star its shape.

The common sea star has many tiny tube feet on its legs. It wraps around a clam, attaches its tubes, and pulls hard at each shell. The strength of the sea star is greater than that of the muscle holding the clam shell closed. Eventually, a small opening appears— hardly wide enough to slip a piece of paper into. But that is all the sea star needs. It slips its stomach out through its mouth and into the opening.

It's hard for us to imagine a stomach that goes out to eat, but this is normal for the sea star. Once the clam is fully digested, the sea star pulls its stomach back in and goes in search of another bivalve.

All the creatures of the sea have developed their own ways of getting food. Food in the sea may swim away, float away, hide in the sand or weeds, or pro-

*On Sanibel Island off Florida's Gulf coast, horseshoe crabs use their pincer-tipped legs to search for food in shallow waters. (James Rowan)*

*Gripping with the many tiny tube feet on its legs, a sea star wraps around a clam, attaches its tubes, and pulls hard at each shell. (Jeff Rotman)*

tect itself with hard shells. Whatever it is and wherever it is, it is still food for some other creature, and it, too, must eat. Eating habits of sea creatures may seem strange to us, but in the watery world of the sea, these habits are perfectly natural.

# Appendix A: Learning More About Sea Life

The following activities will help you learn more about sea life. Choose one or more to begin working on today.

   **1. Begin a collection of sea life.** Seashells, dried starfish, crab claws, skeletons of fish or sea urchins, and pieces of coral are some of the things you can include in it. You can also include seaweeds. Float small pieces of seaweed in a basin of water and lift them out onto a flat, plain sheet of paper. Let them dry, then cover with waxed paper or plastic wrap and tape along the edges. Use small boxes or jars to hold the other specimens. Label each item with its name and the date and place it was found. You may have to visit the library to find a book that will help you learn the names of some specimens. You can find your own items, ask friends to send them to you, or purchase them. Try to learn what foods each of the sea creatures eat. Add this and any other interesting information you learn to the labels or to note cards that you keep with your collection.

   **2. Begin a sea life scrapbook.** Look for articles and pictures of sea life in newspapers and magazines. Get permission to cut them out and paste them in your scrapbook. Draw your own pictures or take photographs if you visit a seashore, a zoo, or an aquarium that has examples of sea life. You can also include information from books. Make a copy of the pages on a copy machine, or write the information in your own words. You may place a thin piece of paper over interesting pictures and trace them for your scrapbook if you are careful not to mark the book. (Of course, you would never cut anything out of a book!)

**3. Make a list of sea foods that people eat.** Cookbooks and menus in restaurants are good places to find ideas. Put a check by the ones you like to eat. Find out what each of the sea creatures on your list eats. Which are herbivorous, omnivorous, or carnivorous? How far along on the food chain is each?

**4. Visit a saltwater or freshwater aquarium.** Maybe you have your own, or at least a goldfish bowl. Watch the fish eat. Are they gulpers? How do they grab the food? Do they swallow it all or spit out some? If there are other animals in the aquarium, observe them closely. How do they eat? Write your observations in your scrapbook or in a notebook.

# Appendix B:
# Scientific Names
# for Sea Animals

Sea creatures, like all living things, have two kinds of names. The first is their *common name*, a name in the everyday language of an area where they are found. An animal often has a number of different common names in different languages. Also, several different animals may be known by the same common name.

The second kind of name is their *scientific name*. This is a Latin name assigned by scientists to identify an animal all over the world for other scientists. The scientific name is usually made up of two words. The first identifies the genus, or group, of similar animals (or plants), and the second identifies the species, or kind, of animal in the group. Sometimes, as scientists learn more about an animal, they may decide it belongs in a different group. The scientific name is then changed so that all scientists can recognize it and know exactly what animal it refers to.

If you want to learn more about the creatures in this book, the list of scientific names that follows will be useful to you. A typical species has been identified for each type of animal mentioned in the book. There may be many other species in the same group.

| Chapter | Common Name | Scientific Name |
|---|---|---|
| **1.** | Quahog Clam | *Mercenaria mercenaria* |
| | Eastern Oyster | *Crassostrea virginica* |
| | Blue Mussel | *Mytilus edulis* |
| | Bay Scallop | *Argopecten irradians* |
| | Atlantic Herring | *Clupea harengus* |
| | Acorn Barnacle | *Balanus balanoides* |
| | Krill Shrimp | *Euphausia superba* |
| | Blue Whale | *Balaenoptera musculus* |
| | Humpback Whale | *Megaptera novaeangliae* |
| | Black Right Whale | *Balaena glacialis* |
| **2.** | Rainbow Parrotfish | *Scarus guacamania* |
| | Common Periwinkle | *Littorina littorea* |
| | Cayenne Keyhole Limpet | *Diodora cayenensis* |
| | Spotted Sea Hare | *Aplysia dactylomela* |
| | Green Sea Urchin | *Stronglyocentrotus droebachiensis* |

| Chapter | Common Name | Scientific Name |
|---|---|---|
| **3.** | Bluefin Tuna | *Thunnus thynnus* |
|  | Atlantic Cod | *Gadus morhua* |
|  | Black Swallower | *Chiasmodus niger* |
| **4.** | Barracuda | *Sphyraena barracuda* |
|  | Great White Shark | *Carcharadon carcharias* |
|  | Cookie Cutter Shark | *Isistius brasiliensis* |
|  | Killer Whale | *Orcinus orca* |
|  | Sawfish | *Pristis pectinatus* |
|  | Swordfish | *Xiphias gladius* |
|  | Atlantic Squid | *Loligo pealei* |
|  | Common Octopus | *Octopus vulgaris* |
| **5.** | Moon Snail | *Lunatia heros* |
|  | Oyster Drill | *Urosalpinx cinerea* |
|  | Knobbed Whelk | *Busycon carica* |
|  | Sea Otter | *Enhydris lutris* |

| Chapter | Common Name | Scientific Name |
|---|---|---|
| **6.** | Goosefish | *Lophius americanus* |
| | Deep Sea Angler | *Cryptopsarus couesi* |
| | Common Worm Snail | *Vermicularia spirata* |
| | Dipper Clam | *Cuspidaria glacialis* |
| | Archerfish | *Toxotes jaculator* |
| **7.** | Giant Clam | *Tridacna gigas* |
| | Three-spot Damselfish | *Eupomacentrus planifrons* |
| **8.** | Electric Ray | *Torpedo nobiliana* |
| | Northern Stargazer | *Astroscopus guttatus* |
| **9.** | Textile Cone | *Conus textilis* |
| | Lionfish | *Pterois volitans* |
| | Moon Jellyfish | *Aurelia aurita* |
| | Lion's Mane or Red Jelly | *Cyanea capillata* |
| | Portuguese Man-of-War | *Physalia physalis* |

| Chapter | Common Name | Scientific Name |
|---|---|---|
| | Frilled Anemone | *Metridium senile* |
| | Staghorn Coral | *Acropora cervicornis* |
| | Brain Coral | *Diploria labyrinthiformis* |
| | Common Star Coral | *Montastrea annularis* |
| **10.** | Sea Lamprey | *Petromyzon marinus* |
| | Cleaner Wrasse | *Labroides dimidiatus* |
| | False Cleaner Fish | *Aspidontus rhinorhynchus* |
| | Man-of-War Fish | *Nomeus gronovii* |
| | Stone Crab | *Menippe mercenaria* |
| | American Lobster | *Homarus americanus* |
| | Horseshoe Crab | *Limulus polyphemus* |
| | Common Sea Star | *Asterias forbesi* |

 *Glossary*

**acid**—used here to mean a strong liquid secreted by some snails and able to soften or dissolve shells

**algae (AL-jee)**—any group of mainly aquatic plants, such as seaweed, pond scum, and stonewart, often masked by a brown or red pigment

**antennae (an-TEHN-ee)**—used here to describe sense organs on the head of small crustaceans

**bacteria**—microscopic organisms found almost everywhere; some types are important in causing dead plants and animals to decay

**baleens (buh-LEENS)**—long, narrow, horny plates that hang from the upper jaw of certain whales and serve as filters to collect food

**bivalves (BUY-valvs)**—shellfish having two shells, such as clams, oysters, scallops, and mussels

**carbon dioxide**—a colorless, odorless gas given off by animals when they exhale and taken in by plants to help make their food

**carnivores (KAHR-nuh-vohrs)**—animals that feed on the flesh of other animals

**cilia (SIL-ee-uh)**—used here to mean the tiny, hairlike projections in bivalves and other animals; they move together in waves to push food particles into the digestive system

**claws**—the strong, curved, pincer-tipped extensions on the front end of crabs and lobsters

**corals**—colonies of sea animals, called polyps, that form hard, rocklike skeletons on the outside of their bodies.

**electroplates**—used here to mean special cells that serve as batteries to store electricity in the electric sea animals

**estuaries (ES-chuh-wair-eez)**—partly enclosed bodies of water where fresh water from rivers and streams and salt water from the sea meet and mix

**food chain**—small animal or plant life becomes food for larger creatures which become food for still larger creatures, creating a support system that links the smallest form to the largest

**flukes**—horizontal tail fins of whales

**gill rakers**—sievelike structures in filter-feeding fish; they trap food before it reaches the gills

**gills**—breathing organs that filter oxygen from seawater for sea animals; for bivalves, they also filter food from the seawater

**herbivores—(HUHR-buh-vohrs)**—animals that feed only on plants

**hypodermic (hy-poh-DER-mik)**—the hollow needles used to give injections, or shots

**mantle**—used here to describe an envelope of skin that lines the shell of a shellfish and covers the soft parts of the animal's body

**microscopic (my-kro-SCOP-ik)**—extremely small in size; an object that can be seen only with a microscope

**minerals**—nonliving substances in rocks, soil, and seawater; certain ones are necessary as fertilizer for plants

**mucus (MYU-kuhs)**—a slimy, sticky substance secreted by some animals

**nematocysts (NEM-uht-uh-sists)**—stinging cells in the jellylike animals; the cells are poison-filled capsules that explode and shoot out a stinging thread

**omnivores (AHM-nih-vohrs)**—animals that feed both on plants and other animals

**organism**—any living thing—plant or animal

**oxygen**—a gas, making up about one-fifth of the earth's atmosphere, that humans and all other animals breathe

**paralyze (PAHR-uh-lize)**—to disable an animal so that it is unable to move

**parasite (PAHR-uh-site)**—often a harmful creature that lives in or on another creature

**pincers**—the nipperlike tips on the claws and some legs of the pinching animals such as crabs and lobsters; used for grasping and cutting food

**plankton**—tiny plants and animals that float in the sea; many are microscopic in size

**predator (PREHD-uh-tuhr)**—an animal that kills and eats another animal

**prey (PRAY)**—animals taken by a predator as food

**proboscis (pruh-BAHS-uhs)**—the long, tubelike snout of snails

**radula (RAJ-uh-lah)**—the ribbonlike tongue of a snail; it is covered with numerous tiny, sharp teeth

**regenerate (rih-JEN-uh-rate)**—to regrow a part of the body that has been broken off; some sea animals can regenerate claws or arms

**seaquarium (see-KWAIR-ee-uhm)**—a sea aquarium, or huge tank filled with seawater in which sea animals and plants can be viewed and studied

**secrete (sih-KREET)**—to form and give off a substance

**shellfish**—animals that are covered with hard shells, such as clams and snails

**siphon (SY-fuhn)**—a tube in some sea animals used for drawing seawater into and out of the body

**tentacles (TEHN-tuh-kuhls)**—armlike extensions on the body of a sea animal; used for moving, feeling, or grasping

**tube feet**—numerous small extensions on animals such as sea urchins and sea stars; used for moving, feeding, and feeling

**venom (VEHN-uhm)**—the poison secreted by stinging sea creatures

**venom sacs (VEHN-uhm saks)**—tiny pouches that contain poison in some of the stinging sea creatures

**volts (VOHLTS)**—units of electric force that describe the strength of the electric current

 *Selected Bibliography*

**Books**

Abbott, R. Tucker. *How to Know the American Marine Shells.* New York: New American Library of World Literature, 1961.

———. *Kingdom of the Seashell.* New York: Bonanza Books, 1982.

Berrill, N.J. *The Living Tide.* A Premier Book. New York: Fawcett Publications, 1956.

Burton, Maurice, ed. *The New Larousse Encyclopedia of Animal Life.* Revised ed. New York: Bonanza Books, 1984.

———, and Burton, Robert, eds. *The International Wildlife Encyclopedia.* New York: Marshall Cavendish, 1969.

Carson, Rachel. *Edge of the Sea.* New York: Houghton Mifflin, 1955.

Earle, Olive L. *Strange Fishes of the Sea.* New York: Morrow, 1958.

Hylander, Clarence J. *Fishes and Their Ways.* New York: Macmillan, 1964.

Jenkins, Marie M. *The Curious Mollusks.* New York: Holiday House, 1972.

Laurie, Alec. *The Living Oceans*. Garden City, New York: Doubleday, 1973.

Meinkoth, Norman A. *The Audubon Society Field Guide to North American Seashore Creatures*. New York: Alfred A. Knopf, 1981.

Migdalski, Edward C., and Fichter, George S. *The Fresh and Salt Water Fishes of the World*. New York: Greenwich House, 1983.

Minasian, Stanley M.; Balcomb, Kenneth C. III; and Foster, Larry. *The World's Whales: The Complete Illustrated Guide*. Washington, D.C.: Smithsonian Books, 1984.

Ommanney, F.D. and the editors of Time-Life Books. *The Fishes*. Life Nature Library. New York: Time-Life Books, 1970.

Zim, Herbert S., and Shoemaker, Hurst H. *Fishes*. A Golden Nature Guide. New York: Golden Press, 1955.


**Articles**

Butler, Michael J. A. "Plight of the Bluefin Tuna." *National Geographic*, August 1982, pp. 220-39.

Clark, Eugenie. "Japan's Izu Oceanic Park." *National Geographic*, April 1984, pp. 465-91.

———. "Sharks, Magnificent and Misunderstood." *National Geographic*, August 1981, pp. 138-86.

Earle, Sylvia A. "Undersea World of a Kelp Forest." *National Geographic*, September 1980, pp. 411-26.

Giddings, Al. "An Incredible Feasting of Whales." *National Geographic*, January 1984, pp. 88-93.

Hamner, William M. "Krill—Untapped Bounty from the Sea?" *National Geographic*, May 1984, pp. 627-42.

Hoyt, Erich. "The Whales Called 'Killer.' " *National Geographic*, August 1984, pp. 220-37.

Neigel, Joseph E., and Avise, John C. "On a Coral Reef, It's a Hard Knock Life." *Natural History*, December 1984, pp. 58-64.

Rudloe, Anne, and Rudloe, Jack. "The Changeless Horseshoe Crab." *National Geographic*, April 1981, pp. 562-72.

Voss, Gilbert L. "Shy Monster, The Octopus." *National Geographic*, December 1971, pp. 776-99.

 *Index*

acorn barnacle, 16
algae, 23, 27, 31, 59, 61, 63
anemones, 72, 75
angler fish, 54
antennae, 18
archerfish, 54, 58

baleens, 19, 20, 22
baleen whales, 13, 18, 19
barnacles, 13, 16
barracudas, 37-38
biters, 37, 42, 44, 46
bivalves, 13-15, 47, 49, 53, 59,
    89, 91
black right whale, 20, 22
black swallower, 34, 35
bluefin tuna, 32, 34, 45
blue whale, 19, 20, 40

cilia, 14, 15, 57
clams, 13, 46, 47, 49, 57, 59,
    85, 91
claws, 86-87
cleaner wrasses, 79, 80-82, 83

cod, 34, 35
cone snails, 68-70
cookie cutter shark, 39
coral polyps, 63, 76, 78
coral reefs, 23, 76, 78
corals, 23, 61, 63, 76
crabs, 34, 44, 46, 50, 52-53, 66,
    85, 89
crawlers, 86

damselfish, 61, 63
dipper clam, 57-58
dolphins, 40
drillers, 47, 53

electric rays, 64, 66
electroplates, 67
estuaries, 58

false cleaner fish, 83
farmers, 59
filter feeders, 13, 16, 19, 22,
    31-32, 37, 39
fishers, 54, 56, 58

flukes, 40

giant clam, 59, 61, 63
gill-rakers, 15-16, 22
gills, 14-15, 22, 32, 35, 57, 61,
    80, 82
goosefish, 54-56
grazers, 23, 27, 29, 31
great white shark, 38
guests, 79, 85
gulpers, 32, 35, 37

hammerers, 47, 53
herbivores, 23
herring, 13, 15
horseshoe crab, 86, 89, 91
humpback whales, 20
hypodermic needles, 70

jellyfish, 72-73

killer whales, 37, 39-40, 44
knobbed whelks, 47, 50-52
krill, 13, 18, 19, 20

krill shrimp, 18

limpets, 27
lionfish, 70
Lion's Mane, 73
lobsters, 44, 46, 86, 87, 89

man-of-war fish, 79
mantle, 59, 61
moon snails, 47, 49, 51
mucus, 14, 23, 57
mussels, 13

nematocysts, 72, 75-76
numbfish, 64

octopuses, 37, 44, 46, 52
oxygen, 15
oyster drills, 47, 49-50
oysters, 13, 49-50

parasites, 79-81, 83
parrotfish, 23-24, 26
periwinkles, 26-27

pinchers, 86
plankton, 23, 15-16, 18, 22,
   31, 57, 59, 72
poisoners, 68, 78
Portuguese man-of-war, 72,
   75, 83, 85
predators, 37, 68
proboscis, 49-52

radula, 26-27, 29, 49, 69
red jelly, 73
regeneration, 44
rockfish, 70

sawfish, 37, 40, 42
scallops, 13
scorpionfish, 68, 70
seabirds, 40, 56
sea hares, 23, 28-29
sea lamprey, 79-80
sea lion, 40
seals, 40
sea otters, 47, 52-53
seaquariums, 39

sea star, 85
sea urchins, 23, 29, 31, 52-53
seaweed, 23, 26, 28, 29, 31, 54,
   86
sharks, 26, 37
shellfish, 46, 52
shockers, 64
shrimp, 34
siphons, 57
slashers, 37, 42, 46
snails, 23, 26-28, 46, 49, 56, 70
squid, 37, 42-44
stargazers, 64, 66
stone crab, 86-87
stonefish, 70
swordfish, 37, 42

tentacles, 27, 29, 43, 68, 72-
   73, 75, 76, 78, 83
torpedo, 64
tube feet, 29, 31

venom sacs, 68, 70

worm snails, 54, 56

 *About the Author*

Jean Sibbald's interest in sea life started in childhood when, as the daughter of a marine biologist, she grew up on a marine biological station. Although her career has taken other directions since then, she was and is an avid amateur conchologist.

*Strange Eating Habits of Sea Creatures*, says the author, "presents a different perspective of sea life. The book describes the most time and energy consuming activity of sea creatures—the search for food. Young readers will not only learn fascinating facts about sea animals, but will also gain an understanding of the interdependence of the various forms of life. They will learn, too, of the special adaptations each creature has made to enable it to reach the food it needs."

Ms. Sibbald's educational background includes an undergraduate major in biology and a bachelor's and master's degree in speech communication. Currently she is a district staff development and training manager for the Florida Department of Health and Rehabilitative Services. The mother of two children, she lives in Tampa, Florida.